C O L L A T E R A L
DAMAGE

By
TARIQ ALI
HOWARD BRENTON
ANDY DE LA TOUR

PLAYS

First published in 1999 by Oberon Books Ltd.
(incorporating Absolute Classics)
521 Caledonian Road, London N7 9RH

Tel: 0171 607 3637 / Fax: 0171 607 3629

e-mail: oberon.books@btinternet.com

A catalogue record for this book is available from the British Library.

ISBN 1 84002 126 8

CHARACTERS

DANIEL

LEONIE

Collateral Damage was first performed at the Tricycle Theatre, London, on 19 May 1999 with the following cast:

DANIEL Jeremy Clyde
LEONIE Susan Wooldridge

Director: Andy de la Tour
Designer: Jill Muirhead
Lighting Designer: Chris Truter
Assistant Director: Thomas Conway
Production Manager: Shaz McGee

For the Tricycle Theatre:
Director: Nicolas Kent
General Manager: Mary Lauder

*A dining table. Twelve places. DANIEL and LEONIE celebrating
DANIEL's 50th birthday with a few friends due in an hour. LEONIE
is sorting out the place names. DANIEL is organising the wine.*

DANIEL: I thought rosé with the asparagus.

LEONIE: Daring.

DANIEL: Petit Chablis then.

LEONIE: I'm putting Heidi next to Joyce.

DANIEL: I thought it was boy/girl, boy/girl?

LEONIE: Yes but what about Tim and Peter? You're so old-fashioned.

*DANIEL goes to put the chablis in the fridge. Phone rings. LEONIE
answers it.*

LEONIE: Hello. Oh hi. Oh. Oh, dear. Oh well never mind. No of
course not, you just get better. Lots of vitamin C. Daniel swears
by ginseng. Yes, you take care now. Be in touch very soon. Bye
now. (*Hangs up.*) Marina and thing aren't coming, they've
obviously got somewhere more interesting go.

DANIEL: Is it you or me thing hates?

LEONIE: You marginally. Twelve was always a squeeze.

She takes away the surplus cutlery, etc.

LEONIE: (*Looks at dish.*) The dishwasher's rubbing off the pattern.
We bought these in Provence.

DANIEL: That market, d'you remember?

LEONIE: Lucy got lost. You started shouting at that postman.

DANIEL: I thought he was a policeman.

LEONIE: He didn't understand English anyway. It says it won't on the packet.

DANIEL: Why don't we try the non-biological tablets?

LEONIE: They'd degrade the crockery too probably.

DANIEL: I'll put the potatoes in. Mashed with celeriac, yes?

LEONIE: It's your speciality.

DANIEL goes. Phone rings again. LEONIE answers it.

LEONIE: Hello. No, no, eight-thirty will be fine. It's asparagus. Then John Dory. No, that's the fish, the recipe's Daniel's. Well, you know, why not? No, no, don't bother, we've got wine aplenty. See you later.

She hangs up. The sound of Channel 4 news jingle from the kitchen. LEONIE carries on with place names. After a few moments.

DANIEL: (*Off.*) Oh God no.

LEONIE ignores him and carries on getting the table ready.

DANIEL: (*Off.*) For heaven's sake.

LEONIE sneaks a taste of a crudite in the dip.

DANIEL: (*Off.*) Why? Why?

LEONIE licks the spoon and puts it back on the table. DANIEL appears in the doorway.

LEONIE: What's happened? Has the marinade gone off?

DANIEL: They're just standing there.

LEONIE: Who's standing there?

DANIEL: Women, children, old men... thousands of them. Just standing there.

LEONIE: Dreadful. We should have been prepared for the refugees. Tents, food, everything.

DANIEL: If we'd prepared too much, it would only have encouraged the Serbs.

LEONIE: Oh I don't know.

DANIEL: Well, we can't leave them there. Everyone's going to have to take some. Thousands. Germany, Norway, Spain.

LEONIE: We could take six easily.

DANIEL: Six thousand? More, more. I think we should take at least ten thousand.

LEONIE: No I meant six. Here.

DANIEL: Here? In the house?

LEONIE: Why not?

DANIEL: You mean, here in our house?

LEONIE: Yes in the basement.

DANIEL: But – but –

LEONIE: Well the kids' rooms are empty.

DANIEL: Yeah but that's the only way into the garden.

LEONIE: We could have a tent in the garden. For another six or so. We could have 12. They're big families.

DANIEL: But – but what about ...

LEONIE: About what?

DANIEL: The language. And there's no bathroom down there.

LEONIE: There aren't any bathrooms on the border.

DANIEL: You know what I mean.

LEONIE: Of course I do. But we could actually do something. We could take a couple of families, they'd be very comfortable down there.

DANIEL: You're quite right, Leonie. I was reacting selfishly. But you do realise they've got to go back home, they shouldn't be taken too far from the region. You see, if they were all moved too far away, the ethnic cleansers would have won.

LEONIE: I thought you wanted us to take at least ten thousand.

DANIEL: Yes but not permanently. Not in people's comfortable homes. They'll be better off in closed-down hospital wards or underused asylums. Where the council can look after them properly. After all, they'll have to be sent back at some point.

LEONIE: Refugees never go back.

He looks at her momentarily and then goes back to the news. Phone rings. LEONIE answers it.

LEONIE: Hello. Oh Max, hi. Yeah. Yeah. Yes, Annabel is coming. Oh. Oh I see. Right. What if I put you at opposite ends of the table? But I thought Sheila knew. Oh she does know? What's the problem then? (*Pause*.) Annabel's bringing her new friend, she's hardly likely to mention it. (*Pause*.) He's lovely, he's Colombian. Antonio. But I won't put him next to Sheila, that'd be asking for trouble. He's gorgeous. (*Pause*.) Fish. See you at eight.

She hangs up and rearranges the place names.

(*Loud*.) Sheila does know about Annabel, you were right. I'll have to put Max next to Tim and that leaves Joyce next to Antonio. He doesn't speak a word of English but Joyce does speak Italian. They'll muddle through.

DANIEL comes in, visibly shaken. LEONIE notices.

LEONIE: What's the matter?

DANIEL: It's on our doorstep. Madness. Malignancy.

LEONIE: Who'd have thought it? In Europe. At the end of the century.

DANIEL: And yet it seems so remote. A war you can turn on and off, like a TV show. I'm so scared we're all just going to get bored with it.

LEONIE: Yeah. Like the Iraq thing. I mean, who knows what's going on there?

DANIEL: Exactly. Imagine if Serbia bombed the BBC, that would wake everybody up.

LEONIE: I know. Some people don't think it's a real war.

DANIEL: It's a real war all right. How many thousands are buried in mass graves down there?

LEONIE: How many more kids are going to die?

DANIEL: Homes destroyed.

LEONIE: Communities wrecked.

DANIEL: Families broken.

LEONIE: Environment poisoned.

DANIEL: God, it's good to talk.

LEONIE: Not too serious for your birthday I hope.

DANIEL: Fifty. Who'd have thought it?

She laughs.

LEONIE: Happy birthday.

She kisses him. Passionately.

LEONIE: I've got a little present for you later. When they've all gone.

DANIEL: There isn't time now, is there?

LEONIE: (*Disappointed.*) I've got to mouli the mustard-seed sauce.

DANIEL: We're doing all right now, aren't we? God knows we
nearly blew it.

LEONIE: But we didn't, Dan. It feels new again. Like 20 years ago.
Shall we tell the others?

DANIEL: Tonight?

LEONIE: They'll be relieved they don't have to worry about us
anymore.

DANIEL: Great. If we're pissed enough we'll take our marriage
vows again. You know something, Leonie. My juices are really
going. I feel revived. It's a terrible thought but it's almost like
this awful war, it's bringing us closer. All of us. You and me too.

LEONIE: That's what they say about the Blitz, isn't it? Hey. D'you
reckon they're having cups o'tea, sing-songs and nookie in those
Belgrade bomb shelters?

DANIEL: Hardly. I'm going to open that now. White burgundy
needs to breathe.

He goes to open the white wine.

LEONIE: Is Heidi still drinking or not?

DANIEL: No, not since she came out.

DANIEL pours two glasses.

DANIEL: One before they come?

LEONIE: Why not?

He pours two glasses and hands her one.

DANIEL: Here's to us.

They drink.

LEONIE: To us.

DANIEL: Next stop Belgrade.

LEONIE looks at him. Somewhat shocked.

LEONIE: What?

DANIEL: Has to be.

LEONIE: What do you mean?

DANIEL: Well we've got to go all the way obviously.

LEONIE: All they way where?

DANIEL: To the end. You can't leave the job half done.

LEONIE: What job? What are you talking about?

DANIEL: You've got to stand up to bullies. Dictators can't win.

LEONIE: Dan. Are you telling me you actually support the bombing?

DANIEL: Of course. Don't you?

LEONIE: Of course I don't. Whatever made you think that?

DANIEL: I assumed it, naturally. Oh my God, does this mean you're against it?

LEONIE: Yes. I am. Against it. Vehemently.

DANIEL: In heaven's name, why? What about the poor Kosovans?

LEONIE: But how does the bombing help the refugees? It's made it ten times worse, everybody knows that.

DANIEL: Yes but we have to face it. It's got to get worse before it gets better. Wars are like that.

LEONIE: My God, that's easy for you to say. You're not standing in a field.

DANIEL: Of course I'm not standing in a field –

LEONIE: No, you're in a comfortable north London house with a large garden which you don't want messed up by a load of non-English speaking Albanians.

DANIEL: You're just being emotional. It really doesn't help. Understandable of course. But when you're fighting fascism there's bound to be initial losses.

LEONIE: How does bombing Belgrade get the refugees back into their homes?

DANIEL: The refugees want us to finish the job. Bomb the Serbs, that's what they say!

LEONIE: They're bound to say that. They're desperate. If someone's burnt your home down, murdered your parents in the back yard, you're going to want them punished, aren't you? It's natural. Doesn't make it right.

DANIEL: Of course it makes it right.

LEONIE: But how does bombing civilians in Belgrade get the refugees back home to Kosovo?

DANIEL: We're not bombing civilians anyway, we're degrading their military machine.

LEONIE: Like the TV station, you mean?

DANIEL: Propaganda's part of their war-game.

LEONIE: Because they refused to show six hours of the BBC every day, we bomb the hell out of them, right?

DANIEL: We're dismantling the apparatus of his war effort.

LEONIE: But the Danube's been poisoned. Hospitals left without power. Homes without water. And the Chinese without an embassy!

DANIEL: Do we really want to argue on my birthday?

LEONIE: No. I'm surprised, that's all. I know. We'll ask Heidi, she's an expert on everything.

DANIEL: Do you want to wreck the evening?

LEONIE: I was joking.

They seem to have finished the row. They get on with the dinner arrangements, glasses etc.

LEONIE: (*Quietly.*) How d'you get to Belgrade anyway?

DANIEL: I thought we weren't talking about this.

LEONIE: I only wondered.

DANIEL puts out some canapés.

LEONIE: The roads in Albania are terrible. Jez and Lucy had to hire mules.

DANIEL: Let's leave the children out of it.

Another pause.

LEONIE: And I'd hate to see Corfu spoiled.

DANIEL: Yeah but we may have to go through Greece. Disembark at Salonika. Move north up through Macedonia.

LEONIE: But what will the Greeks say? There'll probably be a civil war.

DANIEL: Yes, you're right, there is a problem. We could threaten them with the Turks. Give 'em Cyprus. No, you're right, the best option's via Hungary. The terrain's good. Endless plains. And before they know it, we'd have the Vojvodina.

LEONIE: What?

DANIEL: It's where the ethnic Hungarians are in Serbia.

LEONIE: I know that. But they'd all be killed or driven out. Like what's happening in Kosovo.

DANIEL: Belgrade's only to agree to our terms and all this would stop. They've got our number.

LEONIE: Milosevic'll phone you personally to surrender, will he?

DANIEL: He's responsible for this war, you know?

LEONIE: So for as long as he doesn't surrender, there are no limits, right?

DANIEL: He started the killing.

LEONIE: But how many do we have to kill to stop him?

DANIEL: Should the asparagus be steamed yet?

LEONIE: Ten minutes. So how many ordinary Serbs we do have to kill?

DANIEL: It's his choice. All he's got to do is –

LEONIE: – surrender.

DANIEL: Yes. He's a Hitler. You can't compromise with people like that.

LEONIE: So it's about getting rid of Milosevic. Not about helping the refugees. I knew it.

Pause.

DANIEL: I hate this horrible war too. Grant me that at least.

LEONIE: All right, granted. But where does that get us? Anyway I don't think he is Hitler.

DANIEL: What d'you mean?

LEONIE: Why do we always call them Hitler? When we go to war. Saddam, he was Hitler, wasn't he? He still is as far as I know. That makes two of them.

DANIEL: Don't be facetious.

Pause. LEONIE goes about her business.

DANIEL: Remember Srebenica.

LEONIE: Leave it, Dan.

Pause.

DANIEL: Sarajevo. 'Bomb them into madness', that's what they were doing.

LEONIE: Asparagus?

DANIEL: And there's Rwanda of course, remember?

LEONIE: Because we did nothing about Rwanda we're bombing Serbia, is that what you're saying?

DANIEL: At last we're doing something.

LEONIE: Guilt. Milosevic is the bogeyman. Get rid of him and all our past sins are forgiven.

DANIEL: Justice. That's what this is about.

LEONIE: What about justice for the Kurds? I see the Turkish Government's taking twenty thousand refugees. Since they've cleansed out ten times that many Kurds they've obviously got the room.

DANIEL: Two wrongs don't make a right, Leonie.

LEONIE: And East Timor? What about justice for them? It's British weapons still killing them.

DANIEL: Please. This mess is on our doorstep. We're Europeans, it's our responsibility.

LEONIE: You feel guilty, that's why you support the war. You're a decent man, you're upset by the TV pictures, you want to help, it's only natural.

DANIEL: It's not about me. It's about democracy. Human rights.

LEONIE: We're going to civilise the world again, are we? Like Africa a hundred years ago?

DANIEL: This is a just war.

LEONIE: A NATO crusade?

DANIEL: Yes. To stop an evil. Like the Second World War.

LEONIE: Oh we went to war to save the Jews, did we? Not very successful then.

DANIEL: It would have been worse if we hadn't.

LEONIE: How exactly?

DANIEL: You'd be talking German for a start.

LEONIE: The Russians won the war. Everybody knows that.

DANIEL: Beside the point. We went to war to fight fascism. And we won.

LEONIE: Hitler, fascism, genocide. These words are just bandied about. You know why? To silence the opposition. How can you be against the bombing if there's genocide? How can you support the negotiations when you're dealing with a Hitler?

DANIEL: Are you saying it *isn't* genocide?

LEONIE: It's horrible what's going on. But call it what it is. 'Ethnic cleansing' is a crime against humanity. But genocide is the murder of an entire people.

DANIEL: They're dying in ditches and you're playing semantics!

LEONIE: It's not semantics! You debase the memory of the holocaust by calling it genocide.

DANIEL: You know what's wrong with people like you. You still think you're in CND. 'We hate war'.

LEONIE: I'm no pacifist, you know that. There was an invasion once to stop a genocide. A real one. Vietnam invaded Cambodia to stop Pol Pot's slaughter of his own people. And where were the Americans and the British? Denouncing the Vietnamese. Because they'd given the Americans a good kicking.

DANIEL: That's a completely ridiculous analogy. The cold war was at its height and it determined everything.

LEONIE: So it's only genocide when it suits, right?

DANIEL: But if Milosevic isn't a fascist, what on earth is he?

LEONIE: He's a right bastard, no question. He's a brutal, power-hungry nationalist politician and he was damn near overthrown by his own people a year ago. But NATO's bombing might yet turn him into a Serbian hero. On top of that, half the leaders in the region who are supposed to be our side are not much better.

DANIEL: OK he's a fascist like lots of them.

LEONIE: And when the time comes to do a deal you'll stop calling him Hitler. He'll be the guy you can do business with. Just like he was before.

DANIEL: We might have to take him out. Put someone in his place. Who we can do a deal with.

LEONIE: 'Bravo Two Zero'. Macho posturing.

DANIEL: It's not macho posturing. It's a moral imperative.

LEONIE: NATO's holy war.

DANIEL: Don't be ridiculous.

LEONIE: What NATO was founded for? To keep the Germans down and the Russians out. You used to be against that once.

DANIEL: Times have changed. This is a humane war. Being waged by humane politicians. It's not about oil like in the Gulf, it's not the Tories trying to win an election like the Falklands. We have no strategic interests in the Balkans. This time the West means what it says – a war for human rights.

LEONIE: And if you're against the war, you're against human rights, is that it?

DANIEL: Don't twist my words.

LEONIE: And the worse the war gets, the more civilians killed, the more I want it stopped so the more 'inhumane' I'll become, right? You won't foist your guilt on me.

DANIEL: You sit on your moral high horse. D'you think you're the only moderately intelligent person in this country equipped with a conscience?

LEONIE: (*Patronising*.) No.

DANIEL: Don't patronise me. Have you no feelings? Don't you *care*?

LEONIE: *Care*? Oh my God. It's Princess Diana all over again. If you couldn't emote in an orgy of national grief you had a heart of stone.

DANIEL: I couldn't help it, I cried, okay?

LEONIE: Cried? That was only the half of it. You dashed off down the Finchley Road, threw flowers all over the hearse as it went by, you were more bloody upset than when your own father died.

DANIEL: (*Pause*.) Is this argument about us? You're taking it all very personally.

LEONIE: Why do men always assume if we get angry it's about them?

DANIEL: The last time it was, wasn't it?

LEONIE: What? Oh for God's sake.

DANIEL: Well?

LEONIE: I can't believe you bring Jacques up in the middle of an argument about Kosovo.

DANIEL: The personal is the political.

LEONIE: When it suits.

DANIEL: It still hurts.

LEONIE: We fought. We talked. We therapied. We sorted it out. Leave it be.

DANIEL: I'm just saying, it still hurts.

LEONIE: Yes, you're just saying.

DANIEL: Hey, it's my birthday.

LEONIE: Fifty. Like NATO.

DANIEL: I'm sorry, I'm sorry.

LEONIE: If Heidi starts spouting off you're not going to bomb her, are you?

DANIEL: She's never shown much interest in my missile system. (*He laughs.*) Asparagus.

He hurries off. She stops. She's thinking. DANIEL comes back in.

DANIEL: Too much coriander in the marinade.

LEONIE: What I did for us.

DANIEL: What *you* did for us?

LEONIE: I gave up Jacques.

DANIEL: I took you back.

LEONIE: So why raise it now?

DANIEL: I don't know, it just came to me.

LEONIE: You still feel guilty. Making me finish it.

DANIEL: If I remember rightly, the guilt was on your side.

LEONIE: I never felt guilty about him. I loved him. I gave him up for us. Was I wrong?

DANIEL: No. But you were *in* the wrong.

LEONIE: It's always black and white to you isn't it? But life isn't like that, Dan.

DANIEL: Sometimes it is. Sometimes it's stark, right or wrong, make a choice.

LEONIE: One or the other, is that all there is?

DANIEL: In this case, yes.

LEONIE: Sorry, are we talking about us or the war?

DANIEL: Either. Both. Yes. Alright. If you don't bomb, how do you stop the ethnic cleansing?

LEONIE: Call a halt to the bombing, that's the first step. Don't pour petrol on a burning building.

DANIEL: Giving in.

LEONIE: (*Carrying on.*) Get everyone round the table. Especially the Russians, they're the only people the Serbs trust.

DANIEL: It's a pipe dream.

LEONIE: Only a dream because it's never been tried. No-one's interested in making peace down there. Not us, not the Germans, not the Americans. For 10 years all the West has done is stoke the fires of ethnic hatred. Playing off one side against another. Then throwing up their hands in horror when the ethnic cleansers take over!

DANIEL: So who's going to police this Balkan settlement?

LEONIE: International peacekeepers, I don't know, UN troops maybe, but not the people who've been bombing. Then send in massive aid, develop the region. The war's cost billions, that money should be spent rebuilding the place. In Serbia too, who's going to pay to rebuild the bridges?

DANIEL: Not me. I'm not going to go and build bridges for that bastard.

LEONIE: You don't punish an entire people for what their government does.

DANIEL: That's sentimental.

LEONIE: Sentimental? Like sanctions in Iraq – half a million children dead as a result. And d'you think Saddam feels the punishment? In his air-conditioned palace. And the Americans are still bombing and no one gives a damn.

DANIEL: It's a new world now and the rules are different.

LEONIE: Yes they are. Whatever the Americans say, goes.

DANIEL: Grow up. I'm sick of this anti-Americanism for its own sake. Just because the Americans are involved you're against it. A priori. Even if their intentions are questionable, they can still do good.

LEONIE: By accident, you mean?

DANIEL: Why not? Of course they act out of self-interest. Who doesn't? But if they save lives, if they get the refugees back home, who the hell are you to say they shouldn't? Who else is going to stop the killing? Oxfam? CND? The Dalai Lama? You've got to go in hard sometimes. Sort it out.

LEONIE: What is this? Post-socialist third way machismo?

DANIEL: Jesus. Why can't we celebrate being on the winning side for once?

LEONIE: The winning side? Like your precious Gunners?

DANIEL: Always back the losers, is that our duty? The miners, bloody Sandinistas, those wankers in their tree protests, Scampi, whatever his name was. I'm sick of it. Just for once can't the good guys win?

LEONIE: Good guys?

DANIEL: Communism's dead, we've got to get out of the cold war mindset. The Americans – yes even bad old American imperialism – they're so powerful they can even afford to do good. As I said, there's no oil in the Balkans.

LEONIE: Good grief. So it was only the cold war that made the West aggressive, was it? What about before that? The British

Empire – were we so powerful we could afford to do good?
By accident? Is that what we were up to in Africa and India?
Us and the Belgians? Do you know how many 'natives' died
when Belgium 'civilised' the Congo? Eight million. Now
that's genocide.

DANIEL: But NATO wasn't around then.

LEONIE: When did this love affair begin?

DANIEL: What love affair?

LEONIE: You and NATO.

DANIEL: Actually, about the time you were screwing Jacques.

LEONIE: So why didn't you send NATO in to degrade him?

DANIEL: Yeah why didn't I? A few heat-seeking missiles would
have penetrated your fucking lovenest.

LEONIE: But you were smarter then. You opted for negotiations.

DANIEL: Negotiations? What good did therapy do us? Twice a
week with that fat Russian Jungian arsehole. Purgatory. Salved
your conscience, that's all. 'My wife's screwing a frog and I'm
pissed off, there must be something wrong with me.'

LEONIE: At least you're consistent! Talking's a waste of time. Why
didn't you just pack your bags and go? The kids would have
survived. I'd have survived.

DANIEL: Is that what you really wanted?

LEONIE doesn't reply.

DANIEL: Miss him, do you? Hot nights in Bordeaux.

LEONIE: Yes if you must know. Occasionally.

DANIEL: What are you saying?

LEONIE: Yevgeny wasn't such an arsehole, actually. He helped me say goodbye to Jacques. Without denying what we'd had. I didn't have to rewrite history. So yes I do miss him occasionally but I don't want to see him again. So there's no need to feel threatened.

DANIEL: An emotional fudge. That's all we got out of it. We should have sorted it out there and then. Everything cleaned out.

LEONIE: It's the fudge that helped us go on living.

DANIEL: Maybe just living isn't good enough.

LEONIE: So what do you want, Dan, revenge?

DANIEL: I want the memory of that man expunged from my life. Out of my marriage. Out of my house. And out of your head.

LEONIE: Total victory. Nothing less.

DANIEL: A new beginning, Leonie. Isn't that what tonight's about? Our best friends around us.

LEONIE: New beginning, new world order? You're picking over scabs of the past. And how dare you tell me what I can and can't have in my head. That's fascism.

DANIEL: Do you think about him when we have sex? When we have sex.

LEONIE: Maybe I do.

DANIEL: How you think that makes me feel?

LEONIE: Oh go and shag some poor hapless waitress.

DANIEL: Well I just might.

LEONIE: Do. But if you think of me while you're doing it, don't tell me.

DANIEL: You know your problem, Leonie? You're too clever for your own good. I mean, like with this war. Where did you learn all that stuff?

LEONIE: By keeping my eyes open. Reading between the cracks.

DANIEL: No you've been *studying* it, haven't you? To get at me.

LEONIE: Oh please.

DANIEL: I'll give you study. You want to know about this war? This is how we do it.

He rushes at the table and begins to move crockery, wine bottles and cutlery around excitedly.

DANIEL: A four-pronged invasion. A combined NATO force – led by the British. French and German in support – Italians if necessary. Send Apache 'copters into Kosovo behind enemy lines, the US 102nd Airborne – motto 'Death from the sky.' The French paras can go in with them. Behind them ground support via Albania. Blockade the Montenegrin port of Bar – if the Montenegrin government falls so be it. The main strike force goes straight into Serbia across the Hungarian border. On to Belgrade. Southern front prong down here. NATO troops disembark at Salonika, march up through Macedonia into Kosovo to take Pristina. Here. Close on Belgrade from north and south, Milosevic has a choice. Surrender or be flattened. Easy.

LEONIE: Ugly.

DANIEL: Necessary.

LEONIE: Insane.

DANIEL: The world we live in.

LEONIE: And during this ground war, what do you and the rest of your liberal armchair generals think the Russians will be doing?

DANIEL: Nothing. They're broke. What can they do?

LEONIE: Plenty. Arm the Serbs to the hilt. Break the blockade. Attack NATO bases in Italy.

DANIEL: They'd never dare.

LEONIE: You don't know that. The Russians see the world the other way round. The Serbs are their friends. They think Serbia's being attacked to humiliate Russia. Do we expect them to stand by and watch the Americans take over the world?

DANIEL: Yeah, so what? What can they do about it?

LEONIE: They've got a sackful of nuclear weapons for a start.

DANIEL: But the Russians need us. They need billions of dollars.

LEONIE: Unless they see it as a holy war. A pan-Slavic jihad against NATO fundamentalists.

DANIEL: It *is* a crusade.

LEONIE: God. You sound like the fucking Salvation Army.

DANIEL: The world's going to be a better place. Out of the ashes, a safer Europe, a more prosperous Balkans. Look at Germany after the war.

LEONIE: The only way to save them is first to destroy them, is that it?

DANIEL: They're locked in the past down there. Serbs, Croats, Slovenes, Kosovan Albanians, Macedonians, Montenegrins,

Muslims, God knows who else. Tribal hatreds, a permanent cycle of violence. We've got to break it. It's down to us. The West. We can do it. We must do it. It's our moral duty.

LEONIE: I'll blanche the broccoli. Put the table back.

She goes. DANIEL starts to rearrange the table but he is still thinking about the war. Playing soldiers. Moving the 'armies' around. Making quiet explosion noises. Muttering to himself. LEONIE comes back on. She sees the mess on the table.

LEONIE: Dan.

He is silent.

LEONIE: Tidy up, they'll be here in 10 minutes.

He is silent.

LEONIE: I've put you at the top.

DANIEL: It's a terrible mess. Thousands would die. On both sides. How many have been killed already? Hundreds. Can I stand it? I think I can. I'm strong.

LEONIE looks at him warily.

LEONIE: Means you've got to talk to Tim, d'you mind? Ready for an evening of antique wallpaper?

DANIEL: Haven't you noticed? Britain's leading this war. I feel proud to be a member of the Labour Party.

LEONIE: (*Quietly.*) You'll be let down.

DANIEL: We've spent a lifetime knocking our own values. Socialism's dead, Leonie. The project failed. I'm glad. I feel so much better.

LEONIE: Cleansed?

DANIEL: Yes. We were always against things. Carping on the sidelines. Forever whingeing about how even our left-wing leaders weren't left-wing enough. Those days are over, thank God. There's only one game in town and we're part of it. Join me.

LEONIE: No!

DANIEL: Let's go upstairs!

LEONIE: No!

DANIEL: Consummate the new order.

LEONIE: No!

DANIEL: Yes! Come over. You'll feel so much better.

LEONIE: Life without contradictions, eh Dan?

DANIEL: Shitting out the last molecule of Marxism!

LEONIE: There's nothing left in you.

DANIEL: I feel renewed.

A pause.

DANIEL: I've been scared of you.

A pause.

DANIEL: Scared you'd leave me.

A pause.

DANIEL: But I'm not scared anymore.

LEONIE: Nor am I.

DANIEL: I'm no longer walking on eggshells.

She begins to collect the dinner things.

DANIEL: What are you doing?

She continues.

DANIEL: Put those things back.

She continues.

DANIEL: I'm telling you. Put those things back.

LEONIE: Dinner's cancelled.

DANIEL: It's my fucking birthday.

LEONIE: There's nothing to celebrate.

DANIEL: Oh but there is. There's lots.

She carries on clearing the table. DANIEL grabs her arm. She wrenches herself free.

DANIEL: Love me.

He grabs her again. A glass breaks. She throws a glass of wine over him. He slaps her. She pushes him away. He grabs her again. He tries to kiss her. She turns away. He pushes her up onto the table. He starts to tear at her dress. She resists, punching him.

DANIEL: Love me, love me, love me.

LEONIE finally pushes him off her and he rolls onto the floor. He gets to his feet. He looks at her with real menace. She is visibly shocked. She picks up a knife. Silence. Stand-off. The doorbell goes. Suddenly there's a chorus of Happy Birthday from the arriving guests off-stage. The action and the song freeze on 'Happy birthday dear...'

END